I0782031

HOW TO PAINT HOME INTERIORS

The Ultimate DIY Guide to Transforming Your Living Space with Expert Interior Painting Techniques, Color Schemes, and Essential Tools

The Fix It Guy

Table of Contents

Introduction

Picture this: you walk into your home after a long, stressful day, and instead of feeling overwhelmed by the dated, drab walls that greet you, you're enveloped by a sense of calm, comfort, and joy. The colors that surround you are not just mere paint on a surface; they're an extension of your personality, a reflection of your style, and a testament to the power of interior painting.

Hi there! I'm [Your Name], and I've been transforming living spaces with the magic of color and the art of painting for [X] years. I've seen firsthand how a fresh coat of paint can breathe new life into a room, turning a house into a home and a space into a sanctuary. And now, I'm here to share my secrets with you.

In this ultimate DIY guide, we'll embark on a journey together, unraveling the mysteries of interior painting and empowering you to create the living space of your dreams. Whether you're a seasoned DIY enthusiast or a complete novice, this book will be your trusted companion, guiding you every step of the way.

But before we dive into the nitty-gritty of preparation, color selection, technique application, and tool usage, let's take a moment to appreciate the incredible benefits of a fresh coat of paint:

1. Instant Transformation: With just a few strokes of a brush or roller, you can completely transform the look and feel of a room, making it more inviting, stylish, and reflective of your unique taste.

2. Affordable Upgrade: Compared to other home renovation projects, painting is one of the most cost-effective ways to give your living space a fresh, updated look without breaking the bank.

3. Emotional Impact: Colors have the power to evoke emotions and set the mood in a room. By choosing the right palette, you can create a space that makes you feel happy, relaxed, energized, or inspired.

4. Increased Home Value: A well-executed paint job not only enhances your own enjoyment of your home but can also increase its resale value, making it more attractive to potential buyers.

But before we get swept away by the exciting possibilities, let's take a moment to assess your space and set some goals. What do you want to achieve with your interior painting project? Do you want to create a cozy, intimate atmosphere in your bedroom? Or perhaps you're looking to make your living room more inviting for entertaining guests?

Whatever your goals may be, this book will provide you with the knowledge, tools, and inspiration you need to turn your vision into a stunning reality. So let's roll up our sleeves, grab our brushes, and embark on this exciting journey together!

By the end of this book, you'll have the confidence and skills to tackle any interior painting project, big or small. You'll be able to transform your living space into a beautiful, personalized haven that reflects your unique style and personality. And most importantly, you'll have the satisfaction of knowing that you did it all yourself, with your own two hands.

So what are you waiting for? Let's get started on this exciting adventure and discover the power of interior painting together!

Chapter 1
Preparation: Setting the Stage for Success

Clearing the Room and Protecting Surfaces

Before you even think about opening a can of paint, there's one crucial step that often gets overlooked: preparation. Skipping this stage can lead to a host of problems down the line, from paint drips on your favorite sofa to uneven coverage on your walls. Trust me; I've learned this lesson the hard way!

In this chapter, we'll dive into the essential steps you need to take to set yourself up for painting success. We'll start by focusing on one of the most critical aspects of preparation: clearing the room and protecting surfaces.

Clearing the Room and Protecting Surfaces

Step 1: Declutter and Remove Furniture
The first step in preparing your room for painting is to declutter and remove as much furniture as possible. This will give you ample space to move around freely and minimize the risk of accidentally brushing up against wet paint. If you have large, heavy furniture that's difficult to move, consider pushing it to the center of the room and covering it with drop cloths or plastic sheeting.

Step 2: Take Down Wall Hangings and Decorations
Next, remove all wall hangings, such as picture frames, mirrors, and decorative items. This will not only prevent them from getting splattered with paint but also allow you to paint the entire wall without any obstructions.

Be sure to label or take pictures of the items as you remove them, so you can easily put them back in their original positions once the paint is dry.

Step 3: Remove Outlet Covers and Switch Plates

Don't forget to remove outlet covers and switch plates! This small but essential step will ensure a clean, professional-looking paint job. Use a screwdriver to carefully remove the covers and plates, and store them in a labeled plastic bag or container to avoid losing any screws.

Step 4: Protect Your Floors

Now it's time to protect your floors from paint drips and spills. If you have hardwood, laminate, or tile floors, cover them with rosin paper or canvas drop cloths. Avoid using plastic sheeting, as it can become slippery and create a safety hazard. For carpeted floors, use a combination of canvas drop cloths and plastic sheeting, with the plastic layer on top to prevent paint from seeping through to the carpet.

Step 5: Mask Off Baseboards, Trim, and Windows

To achieve crisp, clean lines between your walls and trim, use painter's tape to mask off baseboards, window frames, and door frames. Be sure to press the tape down firmly to create a tight seal and prevent paint from bleeding underneath. For extra protection, you can also use pre-taped plastic drop cloths or masking film to cover your windows and trim.

Step 6: Set Up Your Painting Station

Finally, set up a designated painting station in the room where you'll store your tools, supplies, and paint cans. This will keep everything organized and within reach, saving you time and frustration as you work. Be sure to have plenty of rags, paper towels, and a water bucket for cleaning your brushes and rollers.

By following these steps to clear your room and protect your surfaces, you'll create a clean, uncluttered workspace that allows you to focus on the task at hand: transforming your living space with the power of paint. In the next section, we'll discuss how to properly repair and clean your walls to ensure a smooth, flawless finish.

Remember, the time and effort you put into preparation will pay off tenfold when you step back and admire your beautifully painted room. So take a deep breath, put on some music, and let's get started on setting the stage for your painting success story!

Repairing and Cleaning Walls

Before you can start painting, it's essential to ensure that your walls are in pristine condition. This means addressing any imperfections, such as cracks, holes, or dents, and giving your walls a thorough cleaning to remove dirt, dust, and grease. Skipping these crucial steps can result in an uneven, unprofessional-looking paint job that will only highlight the flaws in your walls.

Repairing Walls

Step 1: Identify and Assess Wall Imperfections

Take a close look at your walls and identify any cracks, holes, or dents that need to be repaired. Use a bright light and run your hand over the surface to feel for any unevenness or rough spots. Make a note of the location and severity of each imperfection, so you can prioritize your repairs.

Step 2: Fill Nail Holes and Small Cracks

For small nail holes and hairline cracks, use a lightweight spackling compound and a putty knife to fill them in. Apply the compound smoothly, making sure it's level with the surrounding wall surface. Allow the compound to dry completely, which usually takes about 30 minutes to an hour, depending on the product.

Step 3: Repair Larger Holes and Dents

For larger holes and dents, you'll need to use a patching compound or joint compound. If the hole is deeper than 1/4 inch, you may need to apply the compound in multiple layers, allowing each layer to dry before applying the next. For holes larger than 3 inches in diameter, consider using a self-adhesive drywall patch or a piece of drywall to cover the hole before applying the compound.

Step 4: Sand and Smooth Repaired Areas

Once the spackling or patching compound is completely dry, use a fine-grit sandpaper (120-150 grit) to sand the repaired areas until they are smooth and level with the surrounding wall. Be sure to wear a dust mask and safety glasses while sanding, and use a damp cloth or vacuum to remove any dust particles.

Cleaning Walls

Step 1: Remove Dust and Cobwebs

Using a long-handled duster or a vacuum with a brush attachment, remove any dust, cobwebs, or loose debris from your walls and corners. This will help ensure that your cleaning solution can effectively remove any remaining dirt or grime.

Step 2: Prepare Your Cleaning Solution

In a large bucket, mix a mild, all-purpose cleaning solution using warm water and a few drops of dish soap. For tougher stains or grease, you can add a small amount of white vinegar or baking soda to your solution. Avoid using harsh chemicals or abrasive cleaners, as these can damage your walls or leave residue that can interfere with paint adhesion.

Step 3: Wash Your Walls

Using a soft sponge or a microfiber cloth, gently wash your walls from top to bottom, using light, circular motions. Be sure to frequently rinse your sponge or cloth in the cleaning solution to avoid spreading dirt or grime around. For stubborn stains, you may need to apply a bit more pressure or use a soft-bristled brush.

Step 4: Rinse and Dry Your Walls

Once you've cleaned your walls, use a clean, damp cloth or sponge to rinse them with plain water, removing any remaining cleaning solution.

Be sure to wring out your cloth or sponge frequently to avoid saturating your walls with too much water. Finally, use a clean, dry microfiber cloth or a fan to help your walls dry completely.

By taking the time to properly repair and clean your walls, you'll create a smooth, even surface that will allow your paint to adhere properly and look its best. In the next section, we'll discuss the importance of priming your walls and when it's necessary to ensure a flawless, long-lasting paint job.

Remember, the extra effort you put into repairing and cleaning your walls will be well worth it when you see the stunning, professional-quality results of your painting project. So grab your tools, put on some old clothes, and let's get those walls ready for their new, beautiful coat of paint!

Priming: When and How to Do It

Priming is an often-overlooked step in the painting process, but it can make a world of difference in the final appearance and durability of your paint job. A primer is a preparatory coating that is applied to your walls before the main paint color, serving several important functions. In this section, we'll discuss when priming is necessary and how to properly apply primer for the best results.

When to Prime

1. Unpainted Surfaces: If you're painting a surface that has never been painted before, such as new drywall, wood, or metal, it's essential to use a primer. Primer will help seal the surface, prevent the paint from being absorbed unevenly, and provide a better surface for the paint to adhere to.

2. Porous Surfaces: Some surfaces, such as brick, concrete, or heavily textured walls, are more porous than others and can absorb paint unevenly. Priming these surfaces will help ensure even paint coverage and a more uniform final appearance.

3. Drastic Color Changes: If you're making a significant color change, such as going from a dark color to a light one or vice versa, priming is crucial. Primer will help cover the old color more effectively, reducing the number of paint coats needed and ensuring a truer representation of your chosen color.

4. Stains and Odors: If your walls have stubborn stains, such as water damage, smoke, or crayon marks, or if there are lingering odors, a stain-blocking primer can help seal them in and prevent them from bleeding through your new paint.

5. Glossy Surfaces: If you're painting over a glossy surface, such as oil-based paint or varnish, a primer will help the new paint adhere properly and prevent peeling or chipping.

How to Prime

Step 1: Choose the Right Primer

There are several types of primers available, each designed for specific surfaces and situations. For most interior painting projects, a water-based latex primer is suitable. However, if you're dealing with stains, odors, or glossy surfaces, you may need a specialized primer, such as a stain-blocking or bonding primer.

Step 2: Prepare Your Primer

If using a water-based primer, gently stir the primer with a clean paint stick until it is smooth and well-mixed. If your primer has been sitting for a while, it may have separated, so be sure to mix it thoroughly. Avoid shaking the primer, as this can create air bubbles that will affect the final appearance.

Step 3: Apply the Primer

Using a high-quality brush or roller, apply the primer to your walls in even, overlapping strokes. Start at the top of the wall and work your way down, using a brush to cut in around edges, corners, and trim. Use a roller to cover larger areas, and be sure to apply a thin, even coat to avoid drips or heavy spots.

Step 4: Allow the Primer to Dry

Check the manufacturer's instructions for the recommended drying time, which can vary depending on the type of primer, humidity, and temperature. In general, most primers will dry to the touch within 30 minutes to an hour but may require several hours before they are ready to be painted over.

Step 5: Sand and Clean (if necessary)

Once the primer is completely dry, examine your walls for any imperfections, such as brushstrokes, drips, or uneven areas. If needed, gently sand these areas with a fine-grit sandpaper (220-grit or higher) until smooth. Wipe away any dust with a clean, damp cloth and allow the surface to dry before painting.

By understanding when and how to prime your walls properly, you'll create a strong foundation for your paint and ensure a beautiful, long-lasting finish. In the next chapter, we'll dive into the exciting world of color selection and help you choose the perfect palette for your space.

Remember, priming may add an extra step to your painting process, but it's an investment in the quality and durability of your paint job. So take your time, choose the right primer, and apply it with care – your walls will thank you for it!

Chapter 2
Color Selection: Choosing the Perfect Palette
Understanding Color Psychology and Mood

Selecting the right colors for your interior painting project is one of the most exciting and creative aspects of the process, but it can also be one of the most daunting. The colors you choose will set the tone for your entire space, influencing the mood, atmosphere, and overall aesthetic. In this section, we'll explore the world of color psychology and help you understand how different colors can affect your emotions and well-being.

Understanding Color Psychology and Mood

Color psychology is the study of how different colors can impact human behavior, emotions, and perceptions. By understanding the psychological effects of various colors, you can make informed decisions when selecting your palette and create a space that reflects your desired mood and energy.

1. Red: Associated with passion, energy, and excitement, red is a bold, stimulating color that can increase heart rate and evoke feelings of warmth and intensity. In interior design, red is often used as an accent color to add drama and visual interest.

2. Orange: Often associated with creativity, enthusiasm, and adventure, orange is an energetic, playful color that can evoke feelings of warmth and comfort. It's a great choice for spaces where you want to encourage social interaction and lively conversation.

3. Yellow: Known for its association with happiness, optimism, and mental clarity, yellow is an uplifting, cheerful color that can brighten any space. However, it's important to use yellow sparingly, as too much can be overwhelming and may lead to feelings of anxiety.

4. Green: Representing growth, harmony, and balance, green is a calming, refreshing color that can evoke feelings of peace and tranquility. It's an excellent choice for bedrooms, home offices, and other spaces where you want to promote relaxation and focus.

5. Blue: Associated with trust, loyalty, and serenity, blue is a soothing, calming color that can help reduce stress and promote feelings of relaxation. It's a popular choice for bedrooms, bathrooms, and other spaces where you want to create a peaceful, restful atmosphere.

6. Purple: Often associated with creativity, luxury, and spirituality, purple is a rich, sophisticated color that can add depth and drama to any space. It's a great choice for accent walls, dining rooms, and other areas where you want to create a sense of elegance and creativity.

7. Neutrals (White, Gray, Beige): Neutral colors are versatile, timeless, and can serve as a backdrop for bolder accent colors. They can help create a sense of space, light, and cleanliness, making them popular choices for modern, minimalist interiors.

When selecting your color palette, consider the following tips:

1. Consider the function of the room: Different colors are better suited for different purposes. For example, calming blues and greens may be better for bedrooms, while energetic yellows and oranges may be better for kitchens and living areas.

2. Think about the mood you want to create: Do you want your space to feel cozy and intimate, or open and airy? Your color choices can help you achieve the desired mood and atmosphere.

3. Take lighting into account: Natural and artificial lighting can significantly impact how colors appear in your space. Be sure to test your color choices in various lighting conditions before making a final decision.

4. Use the 60-30-10 rule: As a general guideline, use 60% of a dominant color (usually a neutral), 30% of a secondary color, and 10% of an accent color to create a balanced, harmonious palette.

By understanding color psychology and carefully considering your palette, you can create a space that not only looks beautiful but also feels inviting, comfortable, and perfectly suited to your unique style and needs. In the next section, we'll discuss how lighting and room size can influence your color choices and help you make the best decisions for your space.

Remember, color is a powerful tool in interior design, and the choices you make can have a profound impact on your daily life. So take your time, experiment with different combinations, and trust your instincts – the perfect palette is waiting to be discovered!

Considering Lighting and Room Size

When selecting colors for your interior painting project, it's essential to consider two key factors that can greatly influence the appearance and impact of your chosen palette: lighting and room size. By understanding how these elements interact with color, you can make informed decisions that will help you create a cohesive, comfortable, and visually appealing space.

Lighting

The type and amount of lighting in a room can significantly affect how colors appear and how they make you feel. There are three main types of lighting to consider:

1. Natural Lighting: Sunlight can dramatically change the appearance of colors throughout the day. North-facing rooms tend to have cooler, bluer light, while south-facing rooms have warmer, yellower light. East-facing rooms have bright, warm light in the morning and cooler light in the afternoon, while west-facing rooms have cooler light in the morning and warm, golden light in the afternoon.

2. Artificial Lighting: The type of artificial lighting you use can also impact color perception. Incandescent bulbs emit a warm, yellowish light that can make colors appear softer and cozier. Fluorescent bulbs, on the other hand, emit a cooler, bluer light that can make colors appear harsher and less inviting. LED bulbs come in a range of color temperatures, from warm to cool, allowing you to customize the lighting to suit your color palette.

3. Reflectance: The amount of light a color reflects can also influence its appearance. Lighter colors reflect more light, making a space feel brighter and more open, while darker colors absorb light, creating a more intimate, cozy atmosphere.

To select colors that work well with your room's lighting, consider the following tips:

1. Observe your space at different times of day: Notice how the colors in your room change throughout the day as the natural light shifts. This can help you choose colors that look great in all lighting conditions.

2. Consider the function of the room: If you're painting a space that relies primarily on artificial lighting, such as a basement or a room with small windows, choose colors that work well with the type of lighting you plan to use.

3. Test your colors: Before committing to a color, paint a large sample on your wall and observe it under different lighting conditions. This will give you a better sense of how the color will look in your space.

Room Size

The size of a room can also play a significant role in your color choices. Color can be used to create the illusion of a larger or smaller space, depending on your goals and preferences.

1. Small Rooms: If you want to make a small room feel larger and more open, consider using lighter, cooler colors such as pale blues, greens, and grays. These colors can help reflect light and create a sense of space. Avoid using dark, heavy colors, which can make a small room feel cramped and overwhelming.

2. Large Rooms: In larger rooms, you have more flexibility to experiment with bolder, darker colors. Warm, rich colors like deep reds, oranges, and browns can help create a sense of intimacy and coziness in a large space. However, be careful not to overdo it, as too much dark color can make a room feel heavy and oppressive.

3. Ceiling Height: The height of your ceiling can also influence your color choices. If you have a low ceiling, using lighter colors on the ceiling can help create the illusion of height and openness. If you have a high ceiling, you can experiment with darker colors to create a sense of depth and drama.

When considering room size in your color selection, keep the following tips in mind:

1. Use color to highlight architectural features: If your room has unique architectural elements, such as crown molding or a fireplace, consider using color to draw attention to these features and create visual interest.

2. Create contrast: Using contrasting colors can help create depth and dimension in a room. For example, pairing a light wall color with darker trim or furnishings can help create a sense of balance and sophistication.

3. Consider the flow of your space: If your room is part of an open floor plan or connects to other spaces, consider how your color choices will work with the surrounding areas. Choosing colors that complement or contrast with adjacent rooms can help create a cohesive, harmonious feel throughout your home.

By taking lighting and room size into account when selecting your color palette, you can create a space that feels comfortable, inviting, and perfectly suited to your unique needs and style. In the next section, we'll explore how to create color schemes and combinations that will bring your vision to life.

Remember, the key to successful color selection is experimentation and trust in your own instincts. Don't be afraid to step outside your comfort zone and try something new – you might just discover your new favorite color in the process!

Creating Color Schemes and Combinations

Now that you understand the basics of color psychology and the impact of lighting and room size on color perception, it's time to dive into the fun and creative process of creating color schemes and combinations. A well-designed color scheme can transform your space, evoke the desired mood, and express your unique personality and style. In this section, we'll explore different types of color schemes and provide tips for creating harmonious, cohesive combinations.

Types of Color Schemes

1. Monochromatic: A monochromatic color scheme uses variations of a single color, often with different shades, tints, and tones. This type of scheme creates a sense of unity and sophistication, and is easy to implement. To add depth and interest to a monochromatic scheme, use a variety of textures and finishes.

2. Analogous: An analogous color scheme uses colors that are adjacent to each other on the color wheel, such as blue, blue-green, and green. This type of scheme creates a sense of harmony and balance, and is often found in nature. To create contrast and interest, use one color as the dominant hue and the others as accents.

3. Complementary: A complementary color scheme uses colors that are opposite each other on the color wheel, such as blue and orange or red and green. This type of scheme creates a sense of drama and excitement, and can be used to create bold, striking contrasts. To avoid overwhelming the space, use one color as the dominant hue and the other as an accent.

4. Split-Complementary: A split-complementary color scheme is a variation of the complementary scheme, using one color and the two colors adjacent to its opposite on the color wheel. This type of scheme creates a sense of balance and sophistication, and is easier to work with than a complementary scheme. To create a cohesive look, use one color as the dominant hue and the others as accents.

5. Triadic: A triadic color scheme uses three colors that are evenly spaced on the color wheel, such as red, yellow, and blue. This type of scheme creates a sense of energy and vibrancy, and can be used to create bold, dynamic combinations. To create a balanced look, use one color as the dominant hue and the others as accents.

Tips for Creating Color Combinations

1. Use the 60-30-10 Rule: As mentioned earlier, the 60-30-10 rule is a simple guideline for creating balanced, harmonious color combinations. Use 60% of a dominant color (usually a neutral), 30% of a secondary color, and 10% of an accent color. This formula ensures that your color scheme is cohesive and not overwhelming.

2. Consider the Mood: When creating color combinations, think about the mood you want to evoke in your space. Warm colors like red, orange, and yellow can create a sense of energy and excitement, while cool colors like blue, green, and purple can create a sense of calm and relaxation.

3. Use a Color Wheel: A color wheel is a helpful tool for creating color schemes and combinations. By understanding the relationships between colors on the wheel, you can easily create harmonious, balanced palettes.

4. Experiment with Tints, Shades, and Tones: Tints, shades, and tones are variations of a hue that can add depth and interest to your color scheme. A tint is a hue with white added, a shade is a hue with black added, and a tone is a hue with gray added. By using a range of tints, shades, and tones, you can create a more complex, nuanced palette.

5. Consider the Room's Function: When creating color combinations, think about the function of the room and how you want it to feel. For example, a bedroom should feel calm and restful, so soft, muted colors may be more appropriate than bold, energetic hues.

6. Don't Be Afraid to Break the Rules: While these guidelines can be helpful, don't be afraid to experiment and break the rules. Sometimes unexpected color combinations can create stunning, one-of-a-kind results. Trust your instincts and have fun with the process.

By understanding the different types of color schemes and using these tips to create harmonious combinations, you can design a color palette that perfectly reflects your style and enhances the beauty of your space. In the next section, we'll explore some trending color ideas and timeless classics to inspire your own unique creations.

Remember, creating color schemes and combinations is an art, not a science. It's all about experimentation, creativity, and finding what works best for you and your space. So grab your color wheel, sample some swatches, and let your imagination run wild – your perfect palette is waiting to be discovered!

Trending Colors and Timeless Classics

When it comes to selecting colors for your interior painting project, it can be helpful to draw inspiration from both current trends and timeless classics. By combining the freshness of trending hues with the enduring appeal of classic colors, you can create a space that feels both modern and timeless. In this section, we'll explore some of the most popular color trends and classic combinations to help you find the perfect palette for your home.

Trending Colors

1. Earthy Neutrals: Warm, earthy neutrals like beige, taupe, and terracotta are having a moment in interior design. These colors create a sense of comfort and groundedness, and can be easily combined with a wide range of accent colors.

2. Muted Pastels: Soft, muted pastels like blush pink, sage green, and pale blue are another popular trend. These colors create a sense of tranquility and sophistication, and work well in bedrooms, bathrooms, and other relaxing spaces.

3. Bold Jewel Tones: On the opposite end of the spectrum, bold jewel tones like emerald green, sapphire blue, and ruby red are making a statement in interior design. These colors create a sense of drama and luxury, and can be used as accent walls or in smaller doses through furniture and accessories.

4. Moody Darks: Deep, moody hues like charcoal gray, navy blue, and forest green are also trending in interior design. These colors create a sense of intimacy and sophistication, and can be used to create cozy, inviting spaces like living rooms and home offices.

5. Warm Neutrals: Warm neutrals like creamy whites, soft grays, and honey yellows are a popular choice for creating a sense of warmth and comfort in a space. These colors work well in open floor plans and can help tie together different areas of the home.

Timeless Classics

1. White: White is a classic color that never goes out of style. It creates a sense of cleanliness, brightness, and spaciousness, and can be easily combined with any other color. Use white as a base color and add pops of color through furniture, artwork, and accessories.

2. Gray: Gray is another timeless neutral that works well in any space. It creates a sense of sophistication and elegance, and can be warm or cool depending on the undertone. Use gray as a base color and add interest through texture and pattern.

3. Navy Blue: Navy blue is a classic color that exudes a sense of elegance and tradition. It works well in formal spaces like dining rooms and home offices, and can be combined with warm neutrals like beige and gold for a timeless look.

4. Black: Black is a bold, dramatic color that can add depth and sophistication to any space. Use black as an accent color through furniture, lighting, and accessories, or create a bold statement with a black accent wall.

5. Beige: Beige is a warm, versatile neutral that works well in any space. It creates a sense of comfort and relaxation, and can be easily combined with a wide range of colors. Use beige as a base color and add interest through texture and pattern.

Tips for Combining Trends and Classics

1. Use Trends as Accents: If you're drawn to a particular color trend but don't want to commit to it fully, use it as an accent color. For example, if you love bold jewel tones, use them in throw pillows, artwork, or a statement piece of furniture.

2. Combine Trends with Classics: To create a timeless look that still feels fresh, combine trending colors with classic neutrals. For example, pair a muted pastel with a warm neutral like beige or gray.

3. Consider the Room's Function: When incorporating trending colors, consider the function of the room and how you want it to feel. Bold, dramatic colors may work well in a formal dining room, while soft, muted colors may be better suited for a relaxing bedroom.

4. Trust Your Instincts: Ultimately, the colors you choose should reflect your personal style and make you feel happy and comfortable in your space. Don't be afraid to experiment and trust your instincts when combining trends and classics.

By drawing inspiration from both trending colors and timeless classics, you can create a color palette that feels both modern and enduring. Whether you prefer bold, dramatic hues or soft, muted tones, there's a perfect combination waiting to be discovered.

Remember, the key to creating a successful color scheme is to have fun and let your creativity shine. So go ahead and mix and match, experiment with different combinations, and create a space that truly reflects your unique style and personality. With a little inspiration and a lot of imagination, you'll be well on your way to designing the home of your dreams.

Chapter 3
Painting Techniques: Mastering the Art of Application

Brush vs. Roller: When to Use Each

Now that you've carefully selected your color palette and gathered your tools and supplies, it's time to dive into the actual painting process. Mastering the art of paint application is crucial for achieving a professional-looking, long-lasting finish. In this section, we'll explore different painting techniques and provide guidance on when to use a brush versus a roller for optimal results.

Brush vs. Roller: When to Use Each

One of the most common questions when it comes to painting is whether to use a brush or a roller. Both tools have their strengths and weaknesses, and the best choice often depends on the specific task at hand.

When to Use a Brush

1. Cutting In: Brushes are essential for cutting in, which is the process of painting a clean, straight line along the edges of walls, ceilings, and trim. Use a high-quality, angled brush for better control and precision.

2. Detailed Work: Brushes are also ideal for painting intricate details, such as molding, window frames, and other architectural features. A smaller brush with a fine tip will allow you to achieve a neat, accurate finish.

3. Textured Surfaces: If you're painting a textured surface, such as a brick or stone wall, a brush can help you work the paint into the crevices and achieve even coverage.

4. Touch-Ups: Brushes are perfect for touching up small areas or fixing mistakes. Keep a small brush on hand for quick, precise touch-ups as needed.

When to Use a Roller

1. Large, Flat Surfaces: Rollers are the best choice for painting large, flat surfaces like walls and ceilings. They allow you to cover a wide area quickly and evenly, with minimal brush strokes.

2. Smooth Finishes: If you want a smooth, even finish without visible brush strokes, a roller is the way to go. Use a high-quality, lint-free roller cover for the best results.

3. Textured Finishes: Rollers can also be used to create textured finishes, such as a stipple or orange peel effect. Experiment with different roller covers and techniques to achieve the desired texture.

Tips for Using Brushes and Rollers

1. Choose the Right Size: When selecting a brush or roller, consider the size of the area you'll be painting. A larger brush or roller will allow you to work more quickly, while a smaller one will provide more control and precision.

2. Invest in Quality: High-quality brushes and rollers may cost more upfront, but they'll provide a better finish and last longer than cheap, low-quality tools. Look for brushes with soft, flexible bristles and rollers with a dense, lint-free cover.

3. Load Your Tool Properly: When loading your brush or roller with paint, aim for a moderate amount. Overloading can lead to drips and uneven coverage, while underloading will require more passes and may result in a patchy finish.

4. Use Even Pressure: When applying paint, use even, consistent pressure to ensure smooth, uniform coverage. Avoid pressing too hard, which can cause bristles to splay or roller covers to shed.

5. Maintain Your Tools: After each use, clean your brushes and rollers thoroughly with soap and water (for water-based paints) or mineral spirits (for oil-based paints). Store them properly to maintain their shape and prevent damage.

By understanding when to use a brush versus a roller and following these tips for proper technique, you'll be well on your way to achieving a flawless, professional-looking paint job. In the next section, we'll delve into the specifics of cutting in and painting edges for crisp, clean lines.

Remember, painting is a skill that improves with practice and patience. Don't get discouraged if your first attempts aren't perfect – with time and experience, you'll develop the confidence and expertise to tackle any painting project with ease. So grab your brush, roll up your sleeves, and let's get started on mastering the art of paint application!

Cutting In and Painting Edges

One of the most important skills to master when painting your home interior is cutting in – the process of creating a clean, straight line where two colors meet, such as along the edges of walls, ceilings, and trim. Achieving a crisp, professional-looking edge can be challenging, but with the right tools and techniques, you'll be cutting in like a pro in no time.

Tools for Cutting In

1. Angled Brush: A high-quality, angled brush is the most essential tool for cutting in. Look for a brush with soft, flexible bristles that come to a sharp point, which will allow you to achieve a precise line.

2. Painter's Tape: While not always necessary, painter's tape can be helpful for creating a straight, clean edge, especially if you're new to cutting in or have an unsteady hand. Look for a tape specifically designed for painting, as it will be less likely to bleed or pull up paint when removed.

3. Paint Cup or Pail: A small paint cup or pail with a handle will allow you to easily carry your paint and move along the edge as you work. Look for a container with a wide mouth and a comfortable handle.

Techniques for Cutting In

1. Load Your Brush: Dip your brush into the paint, loading only about 1/3 of the bristles. Tap the brush gently against the side of the container to remove excess paint, but avoid wiping it against the edge, which can cause the bristles to splay.

2. Start with a Steady Hand: Begin by placing the brush about 1/4 inch away from the edge you're cutting in, with the longer side of the angled brush facing the edge. Slowly and steadily move the brush along the edge, keeping a consistent distance and pressure.

3. Work in Short Sections: Rather than trying to cut in the entire room at once, work in short, manageable sections of about 2-3 feet at a time. This will help you maintain a steady hand and prevent the paint from drying out before you have a chance to blend it with the rest of the wall.

4. Feather the Edge: As you move along the edge, use light, feathering strokes to gently blend the paint into the rest of the wall. This will help create a seamless transition and prevent any harsh lines or demarcations.

5. Clean Up Mistakes Immediately: If you do make a mistake or get paint where you don't want it, clean it up immediately with a damp cloth or a small brush dipped in water (for water-based paints) or mineral spirits (for oil-based paints). The sooner you address the mistake, the easier it will be to fix.

Tips for Painting Edges

1. Use the Right Brush: In addition to an angled brush for cutting in, you may also want to use a smaller, straight-edged brush for painting the edges of trim or other detailed areas. Look for a brush with a fine, tapered tip for maximum precision.

2. Paint the Trim First: If you're painting both the walls and the trim, it's usually best to paint the trim first, then cut in and paint the walls. This will allow you to be less precise when painting the trim, as any mistakes will be covered up when you cut in the walls.

3. Don't Overload Your Brush: When painting edges, it's important not to overload your brush with paint. Too much paint can cause drips, smudges, and uneven coverage. Instead, load your brush with a moderate amount of paint and apply it in thin, even coats.

4. Take Your Time: Cutting in and painting edges requires patience and precision. Don't rush the process or try to cover too much area at once. Take your time, work slowly and steadily, and you'll be rewarded with a beautiful, professional-looking finish.

By mastering the art of cutting in and painting edges, you'll be able to achieve crisp, clean lines and a polished, seamless look throughout your home. With practice and patience, you'll develop the skill and confidence to tackle any painting project with ease.

Remember, the key to success is taking your time and paying attention to detail. Don't get frustrated if your first attempts aren't perfect – like any skill, painting takes practice and perseverance. So take a deep breath, steady your hand, and let's get started on creating the beautiful, flawlessly finished space of your dreams!

Achieving Even Coverage and Avoiding Common Mistakes

One of the most important aspects of a successful paint job is achieving even, consistent coverage without any visible brush strokes, roller marks, or other imperfections. However, this can be easier said than done, especially if you're new to painting or working with a challenging surface. In this section, we'll explore some tips and techniques for achieving even coverage and avoiding common mistakes that can mar your finished product.

Tips for Even Coverage

1. Start with a Smooth Surface: Before you begin painting, make sure your surface is smooth, clean, and free of any debris, dust, or loose paint. Any imperfections in the surface will be magnified once the paint is applied, so take the time to properly prepare your walls, ceilings, or trim.

2. Use High-Quality Tools: Investing in high-quality brushes, rollers, and other painting tools can make a huge difference in the evenness and consistency of your coverage. Look for tools with soft, dense bristles or fibers that will hold and distribute paint evenly.

3. Apply Thin, Even Coats: Rather than trying to achieve full coverage in one thick coat, apply the paint in thin, even layers, allowing each coat to dry completely before applying the next. This will help prevent drips, sags, and other imperfections, and will result in a smoother, more even finish.

4. Maintain a Wet Edge: When painting, always work from a wet edge to avoid creating lap marks or visible lines where one section of paint overlaps with another. To do this, start at one end of the wall or surface and work your way across, blending each new section of paint into the still-wet section before it.

5. Use the Right Painting Technique: Different surfaces and paint types may require different painting techniques to achieve even coverage. For example, when using a roller, use a "W" or "M" pattern to distribute the paint evenly, and then fill in the empty spaces with horizontal strokes. When using a brush, use long, smooth strokes in the same direction, and avoid going over the same area too many times.

Common Mistakes to Avoid

1. Not Preparing the Surface: Failing to properly prepare your surface before painting can lead to a host of problems, including uneven coverage, poor adhesion, and visible imperfections. Always take the time to clean, sand, and prime your surface as needed before beginning to paint.

2. Overloading Your Brush or Roller: Applying too much paint to your brush or roller can cause drips, sags, and uneven coverage. Instead, load your tool with a moderate amount of paint and distribute it evenly across the surface.

3. Not Allowing Enough Drying Time: Applying a second coat of paint before the first coat has dried completely can cause the paint to pull or lift, resulting in an uneven, patchy finish. Always follow the manufacturer's recommendations for drying time and allow each coat to dry fully before applying the next.

4. Painting in Direct Sunlight or High Humidity: Painting in direct sunlight or high humidity can cause the paint to dry too quickly or unevenly, resulting in visible brush strokes or roller marks. Try to paint in the shade or on a cool, dry day for best results.

5. Using Old or Low-Quality Paint: Using old, expired, or low-quality paint can lead to poor coverage, uneven color, and other imperfections. Always use fresh, high-quality paint and follow the manufacturer's recommendations for storage and application.

By following these tips and avoiding these common mistakes, you'll be well on your way to achieving even, consistent coverage and a beautiful, professional-looking paint job. Remember, patience and attention to detail are key – take your time, work carefully, and don't be afraid to go over an area multiple times to achieve the perfect finish.

With practice and perseverance, you'll develop the skills and confidence to tackle any painting project with ease, and create a space that you'll be proud to call your own. So grab your tools, pour yourself a glass of your favorite beverage, and let's get started on creating the even, flawless finish of your dreams!

Creating Special Effects and Textures

While a smooth, even finish is the goal for most painting projects, there may be times when you want to add a little extra visual interest or dimension to your walls. Creating special effects and textures with paint can be a fun and creative way to personalize your space and make a bold statement. In this section, we'll explore some techniques for creating unique finishes and adding depth and character to your walls.

Techniques for Creating Special Effects

1. Sponging: Sponging is a simple technique that involves dabbing a damp sponge loaded with paint onto the wall to create a mottled, textured effect. You can use a natural sea sponge or a synthetic sponge, and experiment with different colors and patterns to create a look that's all your own.

2. Ragging: Ragging is similar to sponging, but involves using a crumpled piece of cloth or rag to apply the paint instead of a sponge. This technique can create a softer, more subtle texture that mimics the look of fabric or linen.

3. Stippling: Stippling involves using a stiff-bristled brush to apply paint in short, quick dots or dabs. This technique can create a pointillist effect that adds depth and visual interest to your walls.

4. Combing: Combing involves dragging a special paint comb or tool through wet paint to create a striated, linear texture. You can experiment with different comb widths and patterns to create a variety of looks, from subtle stripes to bold, geometric designs.

5. Marbling: Marbling is a more advanced technique that involves swirling and blending different colors of paint together to create a marbled effect. This technique can be tricky to master, but the results are stunning and unique.

Tips for Adding Texture

1. Use a Textured Roller: One of the easiest ways to add texture to your walls is to use a textured roller cover. These rollers come in a variety of patterns and materials, from simple stipples to more complex designs, and can create a consistent, even texture across your walls.

2. Apply a Textured Finish: Another option is to apply a textured finish, such as a plaster or a sand-based paint, directly to your walls. These finishes can create a rough, tactile surface that adds depth and character to your space.

3. Layer Different Techniques: Don't be afraid to layer different texturing techniques to create a one-of-a-kind look. For example, you could start with a base coat of sponged paint, then add a layer of combing or stippling on top for added dimension.

4. Consider the Lighting: When adding texture to your walls, it's important to consider how the lighting in your space will interact with the finish. Textured walls can create interesting shadows and highlights depending on the direction and intensity of the light, so experiment with different lighting scenarios to see how your finish will look at different times of day.

5. Practice on a Sample Board: Before applying any special effects or textures to your walls, it's always a good idea to practice on a sample board or piece of scrap drywall first. This will allow you to perfect your technique and make sure you're happy with the results before committing to a full wall.

Creating special effects and textures with paint can be a fun and rewarding way to add personality and character to your space. Whether you opt for a subtle, understated texture or a bold, eye-catching design, the possibilities are endless.

Remember, the key to success is experimentation and practice. Don't be afraid to try new techniques and materials, and don't get discouraged if your first attempts don't turn out exactly as you envisioned. With time and experience, you'll develop the skills and confidence to create stunning, one-of-a-kind finishes that reflect your unique style and vision.

So go ahead and let your creativity run wild! Grab your paints, rollers, and texturing tools, and start exploring the endless possibilities of special effects and textures. Who knows – you may just discover a new favorite technique that transforms your space into a true work of art.

Chapter 4
Essential Tools and Supplies: Your Painting Arsenal
Brushes, Rollers, and Pads: Choosing the Right Ones

Before you can start transforming your home with a fresh coat of paint, you need to make sure you have the right tools and supplies on hand. Having the proper equipment not only makes the painting process easier and more efficient but also ensures a high-quality, professional-looking finish. In this section, we'll take a closer look at the essential tools and supplies you'll need for your painting project, with a special focus on choosing the right brushes, rollers, and pads.

Brushes, Rollers, and Pads: Choosing the Right Ones

1. Brushes:
- Natural Bristle Brushes: Made from animal hair, these brushes are best suited for oil-based paints and varnishes. They are durable and can handle the thicker consistency of these products.
- Synthetic Bristle Brushes: These brushes are made from polyester or nylon and are ideal for water-based paints, such as latex. They provide a smooth, even finish and are easy to clean.
- Angled Brushes: These brushes are perfect for cutting in around corners, trim, and edges. They provide more control and precision than straight-edged brushes.
- Flat Brushes: These brushes are best for applying paint to large, flat surfaces like walls or ceilings. They can hold more paint than angled brushes, making them efficient for covering larger areas.

2. Rollers:

- Roller Frames: These are the handles that hold the roller covers. Look for a sturdy, comfortable frame that can accommodate the size of roller cover you need.
- Roller Covers: These are the absorbent covers that hold and distribute the paint. They come in various sizes, materials, and nap lengths (the thickness of the fabric).
- Foam Covers: These are best for applying very smooth, even finishes with minimal texture. They work well with gloss or semi-gloss paints.
- Microfiber Covers: These covers provide a lint-free, smooth finish and are ideal for low-VOC or water-based paints.
- Wool Covers: These are great for applying thicker paints or creating a slightly textured finish. They are durable and can hold a lot of paint.
- Extension Poles: These attachments allow you to reach high walls or ceilings without using a ladder. They come in various lengths and can be adjusted to fit your needs.

3. Paint Pads:

- These are flat, spongy applicators that can be used in place of brushes or rollers. They are best for painting large, smooth surfaces quickly and evenly.
- Paint pads come in various sizes and materials, such as foam or microfiber.
- They are often used for edging or cutting in, as they can provide a crisp, straight line without the need for tape.

Tips for Choosing the Right Tools

1. Consider the Type of Paint: The type of paint you're using (oil-based or water-based) will determine the type of brush or roller cover you need. Make sure to choose tools that are compatible with your paint to avoid damaging the tools or compromising the finish.

2. Think About the Surface: The texture and condition of the surface you're painting will also influence your tool selection. For example, if you're painting a rough, textured surface, you may want to use a roller cover with a longer nap to ensure even coverage.

3. Invest in Quality: While it may be tempting to save money by purchasing cheaper tools, investing in high-quality brushes, rollers, and pads can actually save you time and money in the long run. Cheap tools are more likely to shed bristles, leave streaks, or wear out quickly, requiring more frequent replacements.

4. Take Care of Your Tools: Proper cleaning and storage of your painting tools will help them last longer and perform better. Make sure to clean your brushes and rollers thoroughly after each use, and store them in a cool, dry place to prevent damage or deterioration.

By choosing the right brushes, rollers, and pads for your painting project, you'll be setting yourself up for success from the start. Remember, the quality of your tools can have a big impact on the quality of your finish, so don't be afraid to invest in the best equipment you can afford.

In the next section, we'll take a closer look at the different types of paint and finishes available, and help you choose the right products for your specific needs and preferences. So grab your brushes, rollers, and pads, and let's get ready to dive into the colorful world of paint!

Paint Types and Finishes: Demystifying the Options

When it comes to choosing paint for your home interior, the sheer number of options can be overwhelming. From different types of paint to various finishes and sheens, it's important to understand the pros and cons of each to make an informed decision. In this section, we'll break down the most common paint types and finishes, and help you choose the best options for your specific needs and preferences.

Paint Types

1. Water-Based (Latex) Paint:
  - This is the most common type of paint for home interiors. It's easy to apply, dries quickly, and offers good coverage and durability.
  - Latex paint is low-odor, easy to clean up with soap and water, and resistant to fading and mildew.
  - It's a great choice for most interior surfaces, including walls, ceilings, and trim.

2. Oil-Based Paint:
  - Oil-based paints are known for their durability, smoothness, and rich, lustrous finish. They are often used for high-moisture areas like bathrooms and kitchens, as well as for trim and cabinetry.
  - However, oil-based paints have a strong odor, require longer drying times, and can be difficult to clean up, requiring mineral spirits or paint thinner.
  - They are also less environmentally friendly and are being phased out in some areas due to VOC (volatile organic compound) regulations.

3. Chalk Paint:
- Chalk paint is a specialized type of paint that provides a matte, chalky finish. It's often used for furniture, cabinetry, or accent pieces.
- It requires minimal prep work and can be applied to most surfaces without sanding or priming.
- Chalk paint dries quickly and can be easily distressed for a shabby-chic or vintage look.

Paint Finishes

1. Flat/Matte:
- Flat or matte finishes have no shine or reflectivity. They are best for hiding imperfections and creating a soft, velvety look.
- However, they are less durable and can be difficult to clean, making them less suitable for high-traffic areas or homes with children or pets.
- Flat finishes are often used for ceilings, bedrooms, and living rooms.

2. Eggshell:
- Eggshell finishes have a slight sheen, similar to the surface of an eggshell. They offer a compromise between the softness of a flat finish and the durability of a higher sheen.
- Eggshell finishes are easier to clean than flat finishes and can be used in moderate-traffic areas like hallways or family rooms.

3. Satin:
- Satin finishes have a soft, pearl-like sheen that reflects more light than eggshell. They are durable, easy to clean, and resistant to moisture, making them a popular choice for high-traffic areas like kitchens and bathrooms.
- However, satin finishes can highlight imperfections more than flat or eggshell finishes.

4. Semi-Gloss:
  - Semi-gloss finishes have a higher shine and reflectivity than satin. They are very durable, easy to clean, and resistant to moisture and grease.
  - Semi-gloss finishes are often used for trim, cabinetry, and doors, as well as in high-moisture areas like bathrooms and kitchens.
  - However, they can highlight imperfections and may require more prep work for a smooth finish.

5. High-Gloss:
  - High-gloss finishes have the highest shine and reflectivity. They are the most durable and easy to clean, but also the most likely to show imperfections.
  - High-gloss finishes are often used for accent pieces, furniture, or trim, but are less common for walls due to their intense shine.

Tips for Choosing Paint Types and Finishes

1. Consider the Room's Function: The type of paint and finish you choose should be based on the room's purpose and the level of traffic and moisture it receives. For example, a flat finish may be fine for a formal living room, but a satin or semi-gloss would be better for a busy kitchen or bathroom.

2. Think About Maintenance: If you have children, pets, or a lot of activity in your home, choose a paint type and finish that is easy to clean and maintain. Higher sheen finishes like satin or semi-gloss are more resistant to stains and scuffs than flat or eggshell finishes.

3. Test Samples: Before committing to a paint type or finish, purchase small samples and test them on your walls. This will give you a better idea of how the color and finish will look in your specific lighting conditions and with your furniture and decor.

4. Don't Forget the Primer: No matter what type of paint or finish you choose, always use a high-quality primer before painting. Primer helps the paint adhere better, covers imperfections, and can even help you achieve a more true-to-color finish.

By understanding the different paint types and finishes available, you'll be better equipped to choose the best options for your home interior. Remember, the right paint and finish can make a big difference in the overall look, feel, and durability of your space, so take your time and choose wisely.

In the next section, we'll discuss the importance of ladders, scaffolding, and safety equipment for tackling those hard-to-reach areas and ensuring a safe and successful painting project. So grab your brushes and rollers, and let's get ready to transform your home with the power of paint!

Ladders, Scaffolding, and Safety Equipment

When it comes to painting your home interior, reaching those high walls, ceilings, and hard-to-access areas can be a challenge. That's where ladders, scaffolding, and safety equipment come in. Having the right tools and safety gear not only makes the painting process easier and more efficient but also ensures that you can work comfortably and securely. In this section, we'll discuss the various types of ladders, scaffolding, and safety equipment available, and provide tips on how to choose and use them properly.

Ladders

1. Step Ladders:
   - Step ladders are freestanding ladders with flat steps and a hinged design that allows them to fold for easy storage.
   - They are ideal for reaching low to medium heights and are commonly used for indoor painting projects.
   - Step ladders come in various sizes, typically ranging from 4 to 12 feet in height.

2. Extension Ladders:
   - Extension ladders are tall, non-self-supporting ladders that consist of two or more sections that slide together to adjust the ladder's height.
   - They are best suited for reaching high walls, ceilings, or second-story exteriors.
   - Extension ladders can range from 16 to 40 feet or more in height and require proper setup and stabilization for safe use.

3. Multi-Position Ladders:
   - Multi-position ladders are versatile ladders that can be adjusted to various configurations, such as a step ladder, extension ladder, or scaffold.

- They are a good choice for homeowners who need a ladder that can adapt to different painting tasks and spaces.
- Multi-position ladders are typically made of lightweight materials like aluminum and can support up to 300 pounds.

Scaffolding

1. Rolling Scaffolds:
- Rolling scaffolds are portable, wheeled platforms that allow you to work at varying heights while maintaining a stable, level surface.
- They are ideal for large painting projects that require extensive overhead work or access to high walls.
- Rolling scaffolds typically have adjustable heights and can support up to 1,000 pounds or more, depending on the model.

2. Ladder Jacks:
- Ladder jacks are brackets that attach to two ladders to create a makeshift scaffolding platform.
- They are a more affordable and space-saving alternative to rolling scaffolds and are best suited for smaller painting projects or tight spaces.
- Ladder jacks can support planks or boards up to 20 inches wide and can typically hold up to 250 pounds.

Safety Equipment

1. Safety Harnesses:
- Safety harnesses are wearable devices that attach to a secure anchor point to prevent falls from heights.
- They are essential for working on tall ladders, scaffolding, or roofs, and can be life-saving in the event of an accident.
- Safety harnesses should be properly fitted and adjusted, and users should be trained in their correct use and maintenance.

2. Non-Slip Shoes:
  - Wearing non-slip, closed-toe shoes is crucial when working on
    ladders or scaffolding to prevent slips and falls.
  - Look for shoes with rubber soles and good traction, and avoid
    wearing sandals, flip-flops, or shoes with worn-out soles.

3. Protective Eyewear:
  - Protective eyewear, such as safety glasses or goggles, is
    important when painting overhead or in areas with dust,
    debris, or splatter.
  - Look for eyewear with impact-resistant lenses and a
    comfortable, secure fit.

4. Respirators:
  - Respirators are essential when working with oil-based paints,
    stains, or other products that emit strong fumes or VOCs
    (volatile organic compounds).
  - They help prevent the inhalation of harmful particles and
    chemicals that can cause respiratory issues or other health
    problems.
  - Respirators come in various types, such as disposable dust
    masks or half-face respirators with replaceable cartridges.

Tips for Using Ladders, Scaffolding, and Safety Equipment

1. Read the Instructions: Before using any ladder, scaffolding, or
safety equipment, carefully read the manufacturer's instructions
and warning labels. Make sure you understand how to properly set
up, use, and maintain the equipment.

2. Inspect Before Each Use: Always inspect your ladders,
scaffolding, and safety gear before each use. Look for any signs of
wear, damage, or missing parts, and repair or replace them as
needed.

3. Follow Weight Limits: Pay attention to the weight limits and load capacities of your ladders and scaffolding. Never exceed these limits, as this can cause the equipment to fail or collapse.

4. Maintain Three Points of Contact: When climbing a ladder, always maintain three points of contact (two hands and one foot, or two feet and one hand) to ensure stability and prevent falls.

5. Work with a Partner: Whenever possible, work with a partner when using tall ladders or scaffolding. They can help stabilize the equipment, pass tools and materials, and provide assistance in case of an emergency.

By choosing the right ladders, scaffolding, and safety equipment for your painting project, and using them properly and safely, you can tackle even the most challenging spaces with confidence and ease. Remember, your safety should always come first, so don't hesitate to invest in quality equipment and take the necessary precautions to protect yourself and others.

In the next section, we'll discuss the importance of proper cleaning and maintenance for your painting tools and equipment, and provide tips on how to keep them in top condition for years to come. So grab your safety gear, and let's get ready to take your painting project to new heights!

Cleaning and Maintaining Your Tools

After investing in high-quality painting tools and completing your home interior painting project, it's essential to properly clean and maintain your equipment. Not only does this ensure that your tools will be ready for future use, but it also prolongs their lifespan, saving you money and hassle in the long run. In this section, we'll provide a detailed guide on how to clean and maintain your brushes, rollers, and other painting tools, as well as some tips on storage and organization.

Cleaning Your Tools

1. Brushes:
   1. For water-based paints: Rinse your brushes thoroughly with warm water, gently squeezing the bristles to remove as much paint as possible. Then, use a mild soap or brush cleaner to work up a lather, massaging the bristles to remove any remaining paint. Rinse again with clean water until the water runs clear.
   2. For oil-based paints: Pour a small amount of mineral spirits or paint thinner into a container and swirl your brush in the solution until the paint is dissolved. Use a brush comb or your fingers to gently remove any remaining paint from the bristles. Repeat the process with fresh solvent until the brush is clean, then wash with warm, soapy water and rinse thoroughly.

2. Rollers:
   - For water-based paints: Remove the roller cover from the frame and rinse it under running water, squeezing gently to remove excess paint. If the paint is stubborn, you can use a roller cleaner or mild soap to help loosen it. Continue rinsing until the water runs clear, then squeeze out any remaining water and let the cover air dry.

- For oil-based paints: Similar to cleaning brushes, use mineral spirits or paint thinner to dissolve the paint from the roller cover. Wear gloves and work in a well-ventilated area. Once the paint is removed, wash the cover with warm, soapy water, rinse thoroughly, and let it air dry.

3. Paint Trays and Buckets:
- For water-based paints: Scrape any excess paint back into the can, then rinse the tray or bucket with warm water. Use a putty knife or scraper to remove any dried paint, then wash with mild soap and rinse thoroughly.
- For oil-based paints: Wipe out as much excess paint as possible with a rag or paper towel, then use mineral spirits or paint thinner to clean the tray or bucket. Once the paint is dissolved, wipe the surface clean with a rag and let it air dry.

Maintaining Your Tools

1. Brushes:
- After cleaning, reshape the bristles and store your brushes vertically in a brush keeper or hanging rack. This prevents the bristles from getting bent or misshapen.
- For natural bristle brushes, occasionally condition the bristles with a small amount of brush oil or conditioner to keep them soft and pliable.

2. Rollers:
- Store roller covers in a cool, dry place, either standing upright or hanging on a rack.
- Inspect roller covers for signs of wear or shedding, and replace them as needed.
- Lubricate the bearings on your roller frames periodically with a lightweight oil to keep them rolling smoothly.

3. Paint Sprayers:
- If you use a paint sprayer, follow the manufacturer's instructions for cleaning and maintenance.
- Typically, this involves flushing the sprayer with water or solvent, depending on the type of paint used, and cleaning the nozzle, filters, and other components.
- After cleaning, lubricate any o-rings or seals, and store the sprayer in a cool, dry place.

4. Safety Equipment:
- Clean and inspect your safety equipment, such as harnesses, lanyards, and respirators, after each use.
- Follow the manufacturer's instructions for proper cleaning and storage, and replace any worn or damaged components.

Tips for Tool Storage and Organization

1. Keep Tools Dry: Store your painting tools in a cool, dry place to prevent rust, mildew, and other damage. Avoid storing them in damp basements, garages, or outdoor sheds.

2. Use Organizing Systems: Invest in tool organizers, such as toolboxes, cabinets, or pegboards, to keep your painting equipment neat and easily accessible. Label your tools and storage containers for quick identification.

3. Separate by Paint Type: If you use both water-based and oil-based paints, store your tools separately to avoid contamination. Use color-coded or labeled storage containers to differentiate between the two.

4. Store Paint Properly: Keep your leftover paint in a cool, dry place, away from direct sunlight or extreme temperatures. Make sure the lids are tightly sealed to prevent drying or spoilage. Label each can with the date, room, and color for easy reference.

By properly cleaning, maintaining, and storing your painting tools, you'll ensure that they're always ready for action and will last for years to come. Remember, a little bit of care and attention goes a long way in preserving the quality and performance of your equipment.

In the next chapter, we'll dive into a step-by-step painting guide, taking you through the process of transforming different rooms in your home, from bedrooms to bathrooms and beyond. So grab your freshly cleaned tools, and let's get ready to create the home interior of your dreams!

Chapter 5
Step-by-Step Painting Guide: From Start to Finish

Bedroom Transformation: A Serene Retreat

Now that you have a solid understanding of the tools, techniques, and safety considerations involved in painting your home interior, it's time to put that knowledge into practice. In this chapter, we'll walk you through a step-by-step guide to transforming a bedroom into a serene retreat, from start to finish. By following these detailed instructions and tips, you'll be able to achieve professional-quality results and create a space that reflects your personal style and promotes relaxation.

Bedroom Transformation: A Serene Retreat

Step 1: Preparation

a. Clear the room: Remove all furniture, decor, and window treatments from the bedroom. If you have large pieces that are difficult to move, push them to the center of the room and cover them with drop cloths.

b. Protect the floor: Lay down drop cloths or rosin paper to protect your flooring from paint drips and splatters.

c. Remove outlet covers and switch plates: Unscrew and remove all outlet covers and switch plates, and store them in a labeled bag for easy reassembly.

d. Clean the walls: Use a duster or vacuum with a brush attachment to remove cobwebs and dust from the walls and ceiling. Wash the walls with a mild detergent solution to remove any dirt or grease, and let them dry completely.

e. Repair imperfections: Fill any holes, cracks, or dents in the walls with spackling compound, and sand smooth once dry. Use painter's caulk to fill gaps between the walls and trim, and smooth with a damp finger.

Step 2: Priming

a. Choose the right primer: Select a primer that is appropriate for your wall type and paint. For most bedroom walls, a water-based latex primer will work well.

b. Cut in: Using a angled brush, cut in the primer along the edges of the ceiling, baseboards, and trim. Be sure to create a smooth, even line.

c. Roll on the primer: Pour the primer into a paint tray, and use a roller to apply it to the walls in long, even strokes. Start at the top of the wall and work your way down, overlapping each pass slightly to ensure even coverage.

d. Let the primer dry: Allow the primer to dry completely according to the manufacturer's instructions before moving on to painting.

Step 3: Painting

a. Choose your paint and finish: Select a high-quality interior paint in a color and finish that suits your desired aesthetic. For a bedroom, a flat or eggshell finish is often preferred for its soft, matte appearance and ability to hide imperfections.

b. Cut in: As with the primer, use an angled brush to cut in the paint along the edges of the ceiling, baseboards, and trim. Take your time and create a clean, crisp line.

c. Roll on the paint: Pour the paint into a clean tray, and use a roller to apply it to the walls in long, even strokes. Start at the top of the wall and work your way down, overlapping each pass slightly to ensure even coverage. Apply a second coat if necessary for full, rich color.

d. Paint the trim: Once the walls are dry, use a small brush or foam roller to paint the baseboards, window frames, and door frames. Be sure to use painter's tape to protect the walls and create a clean edge.

Step 4: Finishing Touches

a. Remove painter's tape: Once the paint is completely dry, carefully remove any painter's tape, pulling it away from the wall at a 45-degree angle to avoid peeling off any paint.

b. Replace outlet covers and switch plates: Reattach the outlet covers and switch plates, making sure they are straight and secure.

c. Clean up: Remove the drop cloths and dispose of any used painter's tape, roller covers, and other materials. Clean your brushes and tools thoroughly with soap and water.

d. Rearrange the room: Once the paint is fully cured (typically after 24-48 hours), move your furniture and decor back into the room, arranging it in a way that showcases your new paint job and creates a serene, relaxing atmosphere.

Tips for a Successful Bedroom Transformation

1. Choose calming colors: When selecting paint colors for a bedroom, opt for soothing, muted tones that promote relaxation, such as soft blues, greens, or neutrals.

2. Create a focal point: Use paint to create a focal point in the room, such as an accent wall behind the bed or a bold, contrasting color on the ceiling.

3. Consider the lighting: Take into account the natural and artificial lighting in the room when choosing your paint color, as this can affect how the color appears at different times of day.

4. Don't forget the details: Pay attention to small details, such as painting the inside of a closet or the back of a door, to create a cohesive, polished look.

5. Take breaks: Painting can be physically demanding, so be sure to take breaks as needed and stay hydrated throughout the process.

By following this step-by-step guide and keeping these tips in mind, you'll be able to transform your bedroom into a serene, personalized retreat that you'll love spending time in. Remember, the key to a successful painting project is patience, attention to detail, and a willingness to take your time and do it right.

In the next section, we'll explore how to tackle a living room refresh, using paint to create an inviting, stylish space that's perfect for entertaining and relaxation. So grab your tools, put on some comfy clothes, and let's get started on creating the bedroom of your dreams!

Living Room Refresh: Inviting and Stylish

The living room is often the heart of the home, where family and friends gather to relax, entertain, and spend quality time together. As such, it's important to create a space that is both inviting and stylish, reflecting your personal taste and lifestyle. In this section, we'll walk you through the process of refreshing your living room with a new paint job, from preparation to finishing touches.

Step 1: Preparation

a. Clear the room: Remove all furniture, decor, and window treatments from the living room. If you have large pieces that are difficult to move, push them to the center of the room and cover them with drop cloths.

b. Protect the floor: Lay down drop cloths or rosin paper to protect your flooring from paint drips and splatters. Be sure to tape down the edges of the drop cloths to prevent tripping hazards.

c. Remove outlet covers and switch plates: Unscrew and remove all outlet covers and switch plates, and store them in a labeled bag for easy reassembly.

d. Clean the walls: Use a duster or vacuum with a brush attachment to remove cobwebs and dust from the walls and ceiling. Wash the walls with a mild detergent solution to remove any dirt, grease, or stains, and let them dry completely.

e. Repair imperfections: Fill any holes, cracks, or dents in the walls with spackling compound, and sand smooth once dry. Use painter's caulk to fill gaps between the walls and trim, and smooth with a damp finger.

Step 2: Priming

a. Choose the right primer: Select a primer that is appropriate for your wall type and paint. For most living room walls, a water-based latex primer will work well.

b. Cut in: Using a angled brush, cut in the primer along the edges of the ceiling, baseboards, and trim. Be sure to create a smooth, even line.

c. Roll on the primer: Pour the primer into a paint tray, and use a roller to apply it to the walls in long, even strokes. Start at the top of the wall and work your way down, overlapping each pass slightly to ensure even coverage.

d. Let the primer dry: Allow the primer to dry completely according to the manufacturer's instructions before moving on to painting.

Step 3: Painting

a. Choose your paint and finish: Select a high-quality interior paint in a color and finish that suits your desired aesthetic. For a living room, an eggshell or satin finish is often preferred for its durability and ease of cleaning.

b. Cut in: As with the primer, use an angled brush to cut in the paint along the edges of the ceiling, baseboards, and trim. Take your time and create a clean, crisp line.

c. Roll on the paint: Pour the paint into a clean tray, and use a roller to apply it to the walls in long, even strokes. Start at the top of the wall and work your way down, overlapping each pass slightly to ensure even coverage. Apply a second coat if necessary for full, rich color.

d. Paint the trim: Once the walls are dry, use a small brush or foam roller to paint the baseboards, window frames, and door frames. Be sure to use painter's tape to protect the walls and create a clean edge.

Step 4: Finishing Touches

a. Remove painter's tape: Once the paint is completely dry, carefully remove any painter's tape, pulling it away from the wall at a 45-degree angle to avoid peeling off any paint.

b. Replace outlet covers and switch plates: Reattach the outlet covers and switch plates, making sure they are straight and secure.

c. Clean up: Remove the drop cloths and dispose of any used painter's tape, roller covers, and other materials. Clean your brushes and tools thoroughly with soap and water.

d. Rearrange the room: Once the paint is fully cured (typically after 24-48 hours), move your furniture and decor back into the room, arranging it in a way that showcases your new paint job and creates an inviting, stylish atmosphere.

Tips for a Successful Living Room Refresh

1. Consider the room's function: When selecting paint colors for a living room, think about how the space will be used. If it's a formal living room, you may want to opt for more sophisticated, neutral tones. If it's a casual family room, you can experiment with bolder, more vibrant colors.

2. Create a cohesive color scheme: Choose a color palette that complements your existing furniture, decor, and flooring. Use a color wheel to select colors that work well together, such as complementary or analogous hues.

3. Use paint to define spaces: If your living room is part of an open floor plan, use paint to define and separate different areas, such as creating an accent wall behind a television or using a contrasting color to delineate a dining area.

4. Experiment with patterns: Consider using a patterned paint roller or stencil to create a feature wall or add visual interest to the room. Be sure to test out the pattern on a sample board before committing to the entire wall.

5. Don't forget the ceiling: Painting the ceiling a slightly lighter shade than the walls can help make the room feel taller and more spacious. Alternatively, painting the ceiling a bold, contrasting color can create a dramatic, eye-catching effect.

By following this step-by-step guide and incorporating these tips, you'll be able to refresh your living room with a new paint job that is both inviting and stylish. Remember, the key to a successful painting project is careful planning, attention to detail, and a willingness to take risks and experiment with color and pattern.

In the next section, we'll tackle a kitchen update, using paint to create a fresh, functional space that is both beautiful and hard-working. So grab your tools, put on some upbeat music, and let's get started on transforming your living room into the inviting, stylish space of your dreams!

Kitchen Update: Fresh and Functional

The kitchen is often referred to as the heart of the home, and for good reason. It's where meals are prepared, memories are made, and family and friends gather to connect and refuel. As such, it's important to create a space that is both fresh and functional, combining beauty and practicality in equal measure. In this section, we'll walk you through the process of updating your kitchen with a new paint job, from preparation to finishing touches.

Step 1: Preparation

a. Clear the room: Remove all appliances, decor, and window treatments from the kitchen. If you have large pieces that are difficult to move, push them to the center of the room and cover them with drop cloths.

b. Protect the floor and countertops: Lay down drop cloths or rosin paper to protect your flooring and countertops from paint drips and splatters. Be sure to tape down the edges of the drop cloths to prevent tripping hazards.

c. Remove outlet covers and switch plates: Unscrew and remove all outlet covers and switch plates, and store them in a labeled bag for easy reassembly.

d. Clean the walls and cabinets: Use a degreaser or all-purpose cleaner to remove any grease, grime, or food splatters from the walls and cabinets. Pay special attention to areas around the stove and sink, where buildup is most likely to occur. Let the surfaces dry completely before proceeding.

e. Repair imperfections: Fill any holes, cracks, or dents in the walls and cabinets with spackling compound or wood filler, and sand smooth once dry. Use painter's caulk to fill gaps between the walls and trim, and smooth with a damp finger.

Step 2: Priming

a. Choose the right primer: Select a primer that is appropriate for your wall and cabinet type. For most kitchen surfaces, a stain-blocking, grease-resistant primer is recommended to prevent bleed-through and ensure good adhesion.

b. Prime the walls: Using an angled brush, cut in the primer along the edges of the ceiling, baseboards, and trim. Then, use a roller to apply the primer to the walls in long, even strokes, starting at the top and working your way down.

c. Prime the cabinets: If you're painting your cabinets, use a mini roller or foam brush to apply a thin, even coat of primer to all surfaces, including the backs and edges of doors and drawers. Let the primer dry completely before moving on to painting.

Step 3: Painting

a. Choose your paint and finish: Select a high-quality, durable paint that is suitable for use in the kitchen. Semi-gloss or high-gloss finishes are often preferred for their ease of cleaning and resistance to moisture and grease.

b. Paint the walls: As with the primer, use an angled brush to cut in the paint along the edges of the ceiling, baseboards, and trim. Then, use a roller to apply the paint to the walls in long, even strokes, starting at the top and working your way down. Apply a second coat if necessary for full, even coverage.

c. Paint the cabinets: If you're painting your cabinets, use a mini roller or foam brush to apply a thin, even coat of paint to all surfaces, including the backs and edges of doors and drawers. Let the paint dry completely before applying a second coat, if necessary. Be sure to let the cabinets dry and cure completely before reattaching hardware and reassembling.

Step 4: Finishing Touches

a. Remove painter's tape: Once the paint is completely dry, carefully remove any painter's tape, pulling it away from the wall at a 45-degree angle to avoid peeling off any paint.

b. Replace outlet covers and switch plates: Reattach the outlet covers and switch plates, making sure they are straight and secure.

c. Clean up: Remove the drop cloths and dispose of any used painter's tape, roller covers, and other materials. Clean your brushes and tools thoroughly with soap and water.

d. Reinstall appliances and decor: Once the paint is fully cured (typically after 24-48 hours), move your appliances and decor back into the room, arranging them in a way that showcases your new paint job and creates a fresh, functional atmosphere.

Tips for a Successful Kitchen Update

1. Choose colors that complement your cabinets and countertops: If you're not painting your cabinets, select wall colors that work well with your existing cabinetry and countertop materials. Neutral tones like white, gray, and beige are classic choices that can help brighten and modernize the space.

2. Use paint to create a focal point: Consider using a bold, contrasting color on an accent wall or island to create a focal point and add visual interest to the room.

3. Don't forget the details: Pay attention to small details like painting the insides of cabinets or the backs of doors to create a cohesive, polished look.

4. Maximize functionality: When arranging your appliances and decor, think about how you use your kitchen on a daily basis. Make sure frequently used items are easily accessible and that there is plenty of clear counter space for food preparation and cooking.

5. Add personality with accessories: Once your paint job is complete, add personality and style to your kitchen with colorful accessories like dish towels, rugs, and artwork. These small touches can help tie the room together and make it feel like a true reflection of your personal taste.

By following this step-by-step guide and incorporating these tips, you'll be able to update your kitchen with a fresh, functional paint job that combines beauty and practicality. Remember, the key to a successful painting project is careful planning, attention to detail, and a willingness to take your time and do it right.

In the next section, we'll explore how to tackle a bathroom makeover, using paint to create a clean, spa-like retreat that is both relaxing and rejuvenating. So grab your tools, put on some comfortable shoes, and let's get started on transforming your kitchen into the fresh, functional space of your dreams!

Bathroom Makeover: Clean and Spa-Like

The bathroom is a space where we begin and end our days, making it an important room for setting the tone and promoting relaxation and self-care. A well-designed bathroom should be both functional and inviting, with a clean, spa-like atmosphere that encourages rest and rejuvenation. In this section, we'll walk you through the process of giving your bathroom a makeover with a new paint job, from preparation to finishing touches.

Step 1: Preparation

a. Clear the room: Remove all toiletries, decor, and window treatments from the bathroom. If you have a large vanity or storage unit that is difficult to move, cover it with drop cloths to protect it from paint drips and splatters.

b. Protect the floor and fixtures: Lay down drop cloths or rosin paper to protect your flooring, toilet, sink, and bathtub from paint. Use painter's tape to secure the edges of the drop cloths and to cover any fixtures or hardware that cannot be removed.

c. Remove outlet covers and switch plates: Unscrew and remove all outlet covers and switch plates, and store them in a labeled bag for easy reassembly.

d. Clean the walls and surfaces: Use a mild detergent or all-purpose cleaner to remove any dirt, soap scum, or mildew from the walls and surfaces. Pay special attention to areas around the sink, toilet, and shower, where buildup is most likely to occur. Let the surfaces dry completely before proceeding.

e. Repair imperfections: Fill any holes, cracks, or dents in the walls with spackling compound, and sand smooth once dry. Use painter's caulk to fill gaps between the walls and trim, and smooth with a damp finger.

Step 2: Priming

a. Choose the right primer: Select a moisture-resistant, mildew-resistant primer that is suitable for use in the bathroom. This will help prevent peeling, cracking, and other moisture-related issues down the line.

b. Prime the walls: Using an angled brush, cut in the primer along the edges of the ceiling, baseboards, and trim. Then, use a roller to apply the primer to the walls in long, even strokes, starting at the top and working your way down.

c. Prime the ceiling: If you're painting the ceiling, use a roller with an extension pole to apply the primer in long, even strokes, starting at one corner and working your way across the room.

Step 3: Painting

a. Choose your paint and finish: Select a high-quality, moisture-resistant paint that is suitable for use in the bathroom. Semi-gloss or high-gloss finishes are often preferred for their durability and ease of cleaning.

b. Paint the walls: As with the primer, use an angled brush to cut in the paint along the edges of the ceiling, baseboards, and trim. Then, use a roller to apply the paint to the walls in long, even strokes, starting at the top and working your way down. Apply a second coat if necessary for full, even coverage.

c. Paint the ceiling: If you're painting the ceiling, use a roller with an extension pole to apply the paint in long, even strokes, starting at one corner and working your way across the room. Apply a second coat if necessary for full, even coverage.

Step 4: Finishing Touches

a. Remove painter's tape: Once the paint is completely dry, carefully remove any painter's tape, pulling it away from the wall at a 45-degree angle to avoid peeling off any paint.

b. Replace outlet covers and switch plates: Reattach the outlet covers and switch plates, making sure they are straight and secure.

c. Clean up: Remove the drop cloths and dispose of any used painter's tape, roller covers, and other materials. Clean your brushes and tools thoroughly with soap and water.

d. Reinstall fixtures and decor: Once the paint is fully cured (typically after 24-48 hours), reinstall any fixtures or hardware that were removed, such as towel bars or shelves. Then, add your toiletries and decor back into the room, arranging them in a way that showcases your new paint job and creates a clean, spa-like atmosphere.

Tips for a Successful Bathroom Makeover

1. Choose calming colors: When selecting paint colors for a bathroom, opt for soothing, spa-like hues such as soft blues, greens, or neutrals. These colors can help create a sense of tranquility and relaxation in the space.

2. Consider the lighting: Bathrooms often have limited natural light, so it's important to consider how your paint color will look under artificial lighting. Opt for colors that are bright and reflective to help maximize the available light and create a sense of spaciousness.

3. Don't forget the details: Pay attention to small details like painting the inside of a medicine cabinet or the back of a door to create a cohesive, polished look.

4. Add texture with accessories: Once your paint job is complete, add texture and interest to your bathroom with plush towels, a cozy bath mat, and some greenery or natural elements like stones or shells.

5. Prioritize organization: A clean, clutter-free bathroom is key to creating a spa-like atmosphere. Invest in some attractive storage solutions like baskets, shelves, or a vanity with plenty of drawers to keep toiletries and other essentials neatly organized and out of sight.

By following this step-by-step guide and incorporating these tips, you'll be able to give your bathroom a makeover that is both clean and spa-like, creating a relaxing retreat that you'll love spending time in. Remember, the key to a successful painting project is careful planning, attention to detail, and a willingness to take your time and do it right.

With your bathroom makeover complete, you'll have tackled some of the most important rooms in your home, creating a series of beautiful, functional spaces that reflect your personal style and meet your daily needs. In the next chapter, we'll explore some common painting challenges and how to troubleshoot them, ensuring that your DIY painting projects are a success from start to finish.

Chapter 6
Troubleshooting and FAQs:
Overcoming Challenges
Fixing Common Painting Mistakes

As with any DIY project, painting your home interior can come with its fair share of challenges and obstacles. From drips and splatters to uneven coverage and peeling paint, even the most experienced painters can encounter issues along the way. In this section, we'll explore some common painting mistakes and provide step-by-step guidance on how to fix them, as well as answer some frequently asked questions to help you troubleshoot any challenges that may arise.

Fixing Common Painting Mistakes

1. Drips and Splatters
Drips and splatters are one of the most common painting mistakes, often occurring when too much paint is applied or when the paint is applied too quickly. To fix this issue:
a. Let the paint dry completely before attempting to remove the drips or splatters.
b. Use a razor blade or putty knife to gently scrape off the excess paint, being careful not to scratch or gouge the surface beneath.
c. Sand the area lightly with fine-grit sandpaper to smooth out any remaining bumps or ridges.
d. Touch up the area with a small brush and a bit of leftover paint, blending it carefully with the surrounding surface.

2. Brush Marks and Streaks
Brush marks and streaks can occur when the paint is applied too thickly or when the brush is overloaded with paint. To fix this issue:

a. Let the paint dry completely before attempting to fix the brush marks or streaks.

b. Sand the area lightly with fine-grit sandpaper to smooth out the surface and remove any obvious brush marks.

c. Apply a thin, even coat of paint over the area using a high-quality brush or roller, taking care to blend it smoothly with the surrounding surface.

d. If necessary, apply a second thin coat of paint to achieve full, even coverage.

3. Uneven Coverage and Patchiness

Uneven coverage and patchiness can occur when the paint is applied too thinly or when the surface is not properly prepared before painting. To fix this issue:

a. Let the paint dry completely before attempting to fix the uneven coverage or patchiness.

b. Apply a second coat of paint over the entire surface, taking care to apply it evenly and smoothly.

c. If the issue persists, you may need to apply a third coat of paint or even start over with a fresh coat of primer to ensure a smooth, even base for the paint to adhere to.

4. Peeling and Cracking Paint

Peeling and cracking paint can occur when the surface is not properly cleaned or prepared before painting, or when the paint is exposed to excessive moisture or humidity. To fix this issue:

a. Scrape off any loose or peeling paint with a putty knife or paint scraper, being careful not to damage the surface beneath.

b. Sand the area lightly with medium-grit sandpaper to smooth out any rough edges and create a flat surface for the new paint to adhere to.

c. Clean the surface thoroughly with a degreaser or all-purpose cleaner to remove any dirt, dust, or debris.

d. Apply a coat of primer to the area to help the new paint adhere properly and prevent future peeling or cracking.

e. Once the primer is dry, apply a fresh coat of paint over the area, blending it carefully with the surrounding surface.

Frequently Asked Questions

1. How do I choose the right paint finish for my room?

The right paint finish depends on the room's function and the amount of traffic and wear it receives. Here are some general guidelines:

- Flat/matte finish: Best for low-traffic areas like bedrooms and living rooms, as it helps hide surface imperfections.
- Eggshell finish: Best for moderate-traffic areas like hallways and family rooms, as it offers a subtle sheen and is easier to clean than flat/matte finishes.
- Satin finish: Best for high-traffic areas like kitchens and bathrooms, as it is durable, easy to clean, and moisture-resistant.
- Semi-gloss/high-gloss finish: Best for trim, doors, and cabinetry, as it is highly durable and easy to clean, but may highlight surface imperfections.

2. How much paint do I need for my room?

To estimate how much paint you'll need, measure the length and width of each wall in feet, then multiply those numbers together to get the total square footage. Add up the square footage of all the walls, then subtract the square footage of any doors, windows, or other non-paintable areas. As a general rule of thumb, one gallon of paint will cover approximately 400 square feet, but this can vary depending on the paint brand, surface texture, and number of coats needed.

3. How long should I wait between coats of paint?

The recommended drying time between coats of paint varies depending on the type of paint, the room's humidity and temperature, and the thickness of the paint application. As a general guideline, wait at least 2-4 hours between coats of latex paint, and 24 hours between coats of oil-based paint. Always consult the paint can label or manufacturer's instructions for specific drying times.

4. Can I paint over wallpaper?

While it is possible to paint over wallpaper, it is not recommended unless the wallpaper is in good condition and firmly attached to the wall. If the wallpaper is peeling, bubbling, or otherwise damaged, it should be removed before painting. If you do decide to paint over wallpaper, be sure to prime the surface first with an oil-based primer to help the paint adhere properly and prevent the wallpaper from showing through.

5. How do I prevent paint from drying out between coats?

To prevent paint from drying out between coats, pour the amount of paint you need for the current coat into a separate container, then seal the original paint can tightly with a lid or plastic wrap. You can also place a damp cloth over the top of the paint tray or container to help keep the paint from drying out or forming a skin on the surface.

By following these troubleshooting tips and keeping these frequently asked questions in mind, you'll be well-equipped to handle any challenges that may arise during your DIY painting projects. Remember, the key to success is patience, persistence, and a willingness to learn from your mistakes and adapt as needed.

With your newfound knowledge and confidence, you'll be able to tackle any painting project with ease, creating beautiful, long-lasting results that you can be proud of. So grab your tools, put on your painting clothes, and get ready to transform your home one brushstroke at a time!

Dealing with Difficult Surfaces and Textures

While painting a smooth, flat wall may seem like a straightforward task, not all surfaces are created equal. From rough, textured walls to slick, glossy tiles, different surfaces and textures can present unique challenges when it comes to achieving a smooth, even paint finish. In this section, we'll explore some common difficult surfaces and textures and provide step-by-step guidance on how to tackle them like a pro.

1. Textured Walls (e.g., Popcorn Ceilings, Stucco, Brick)
Textured walls can be tricky to paint, as the uneven surface can create an inconsistent finish and may require more paint to achieve full coverage. To paint textured walls:
a. Start by cleaning the surface thoroughly with a duster or vacuum to remove any loose debris or dust.
b. If the texture is particularly rough or uneven, you may need to apply a coat of high-build primer to help fill in the gaps and create a smoother surface for the paint to adhere to.
c. Use a thick-nap roller (3/4" or higher) to apply the paint, as this will help the roller cover reach into the crevices and provide even coverage.
d. Work in small sections, applying a generous amount of paint and using a brush to work it into any hard-to-reach areas or tight corners.
e. Allow the paint to dry completely before applying a second coat, if needed.

2. Glossy Surfaces (e.g., Tile, Glass, Metal)
Glossy surfaces can be challenging to paint because the slick, non-porous surface can prevent the paint from adhering properly, leading to chipping, peeling, or uneven coverage. To paint glossy surfaces:

a. Start by cleaning the surface thoroughly with a degreaser or all-purpose cleaner to remove any dirt, grease, or grime.

b. Sand the surface lightly with fine-grit sandpaper to create a slightly rougher texture for the paint to adhere to. Wipe away any sanding dust with a damp cloth.

c. Apply a coat of bonding primer specifically designed for glossy surfaces. This will help the paint adhere properly and prevent chipping or peeling.

d. Use a high-quality, semi-gloss or high-gloss paint that is suitable for the surface you're painting (e.g., tile paint for tiles, metal paint for metal).

e. Apply the paint in thin, even coats using a brush or roller designed for smooth surfaces, such as a foam roller or a short-nap velour roller.

f. Allow the paint to dry completely before applying a second coat, if needed.

3. Damaged or Uneven Surfaces (e.g., Cracks, Holes, Dents)

Damaged or uneven surfaces can be unsightly and may prevent the paint from adhering properly or creating a smooth, even finish. To paint damaged or uneven surfaces:

a. Start by repairing any cracks, holes, or dents in the surface using spackling compound or patching plaster. Allow the filler to dry completely, then sand it smooth with fine-grit sandpaper.

b. If the surface is severely damaged or uneven, you may need to apply a coat of high-build primer to help fill in the gaps and create a smoother surface for the paint to adhere to.

c. Once the surface is repaired and primed, apply the paint in thin, even coats using a brush or roller suitable for the surface texture.

d. Allow the paint to dry completely before applying a second coat, if needed.

e. If the surface is still slightly uneven after painting, you can use a paint leveler or extender to help create a smoother, more even finish.

4. Porous Surfaces (e.g., Wood, Concrete, Drywall)

Porous surfaces can absorb paint unevenly, leading to a blotchy or inconsistent finish. To paint porous surfaces:

a. Start by cleaning the surface thoroughly to remove any dirt, dust, or debris.

b. If the surface is particularly porous or absorbent, you may need to apply a coat of primer to help seal the surface and prevent the paint from soaking in unevenly.

c. Use a high-quality, acrylic latex paint that is suitable for the surface you're painting (e.g., wood paint for wood, masonry paint for concrete).

d. Apply the paint in thin, even coats using a brush or roller suitable for the surface texture. For example, use a thick-nap roller for rough, porous surfaces like concrete, or a medium-nap roller for semi-smooth surfaces like wood.

e. Allow the paint to dry completely before applying a second coat, if needed.

f. If the surface is still slightly uneven or blotchy after painting, you can use a paint conditioner or extender to help improve the flow and coverage of the paint.

Tips for Painting Difficult Surfaces and Textures

1. Always start with a clean, dry surface. Any dirt, grease, or moisture on the surface can prevent the paint from adhering properly and may lead to peeling, chipping, or other issues down the line.

2. Use the right tools for the job. Different surfaces and textures may require different types of brushes, rollers, or sprayers to achieve the best results. Be sure to choose tools that are suitable for the specific surface you're painting.

3. Don't rush the process. Painting difficult surfaces and textures may take more time and effort than painting a smooth, flat wall. Be patient and take your time to ensure even coverage and a smooth, professional-looking finish.

4. Don't be afraid to experiment. If you're not sure how a particular paint or technique will look on a difficult surface or texture, try it out on a small, inconspicuous area first. This will allow you to see how the paint adheres and dries, and make any necessary adjustments before tackling the entire surface.

By following these step-by-step guidelines and keeping these tips in mind, you'll be well-equipped to handle even the most challenging surfaces and textures with confidence and skill. Whether you're painting a rough, textured wall or a slick, glossy tile, you'll be able to achieve a beautiful, long-lasting finish that you can be proud of.

So don't let difficult surfaces and textures intimidate you – with a little knowledge, patience, and perseverance, you can transform any space into a stunning work of art. Happy painting!

Answers to Frequently Asked Questions

When it comes to painting your home interior, it's natural to have questions and concerns along the way. From choosing the right paint and tools to troubleshooting common issues, there's a lot to learn and consider. In this section, we'll answer some of the most frequently asked questions about interior painting, providing clear, concise guidance to help you achieve the best possible results.

1. How do I choose the right paint sheen for my room?

Choosing the right paint sheen depends on the room's function, the amount of traffic it receives, and your personal preference. Here's a quick guide:

- Flat/Matte: Best for low-traffic areas like bedrooms and living rooms, as it helps hide surface imperfections and creates a soft, velvety look.
- Eggshell: Best for moderate-traffic areas like hallways and family rooms, as it offers a subtle sheen and is easier to clean than flat/matte finishes.
- Satin: Best for high-traffic areas like kitchens and bathrooms, as it is durable, easy to clean, and has a soft, pearl-like sheen.
- Semi-Gloss/High-Gloss: Best for trim, doors, and cabinetry, as it is highly durable and easy to clean, but may highlight surface imperfections.

2. How much paint do I need for my room?

To estimate how much paint you'll need, measure the length and width of each wall, then multiply those numbers together to get the total square footage. Add up the square footage of all the walls, then subtract the square footage of any doors, windows, or other non-paintable areas. As a general rule of thumb, one gallon of paint covers approximately 400 square feet, but this can vary depending on the paint brand, surface texture, and number of coats needed. It's always better to have a little extra paint than to run out mid-project.

3. Can I paint over wallpaper?

While it is possible to paint over wallpaper, it's not always recommended. If the wallpaper is in good condition, firmly attached to the wall, and has a smooth texture, you may be able to paint over it successfully. However, if the wallpaper is peeling, bubbling, or has a rough, textured surface, it's best to remove it before painting. If you do decide to paint over wallpaper, be sure to prime the surface first with an oil-based primer to help the paint adhere properly and prevent the wallpaper pattern from showing through.

4. How long should I wait between coats of paint?

The recommended drying time between coats of paint varies depending on the type of paint, the room's humidity and temperature, and the thickness of the paint application. As a general guideline:

- Latex Paint: Wait at least 2-4 hours between coats, or until the paint feels dry to the touch.
- Oil-Based Paint: Wait at least 24 hours between coats to ensure the paint has fully dried and cured.

Always consult the paint can label or manufacturer's instructions for specific drying times, as some paints may require longer or shorter drying times depending on the formula.

5. How do I prevent brush marks and streaks when painting?

To prevent brush marks and streaks, follow these tips:

- Use a high-quality, appropriate brush for the type of paint and surface you're working with.
- Load your brush with enough paint to cover the surface, but not so much that it's dripping or oversaturated
- Apply the paint in long, even strokes, working in the same direction and overlapping each stroke slightly to ensure even coverage.

- Avoid going over the same area multiple times, as this can cause the paint to start drying and create visible brush marks.
- If you do notice any brush marks or streaks, wait for the paint to dry completely, then lightly sand the area with fine-grit sandpaper and apply another thin, even coat of paint.

6. Can I use a paint sprayer instead of a brush or roller?

Yes, you can use a paint sprayer to apply paint to your interior walls and surfaces. Paint sprayers can be a great option for large, open areas or for achieving a very smooth, even finish. However, paint sprayers do require some practice and skill to use effectively, and they can be messier and more time-consuming to set up and clean than traditional brushes or rollers. If you're new to using a paint sprayer, it's a good idea to practice on a scrap piece of cardboard or wood before tackling your walls, and be sure to follow the manufacturer's instructions for proper use and maintenance.

7. How do I clean my paint brushes and rollers after use?

Cleaning your paint brushes and rollers properly after each use is essential for maintaining their quality and performance over time. Here's how to clean them:

- Latex Paint: Rinse the brush or roller thoroughly with warm water, then use a mild soap or brush cleaner to remove any remaining paint. Rinse again with clean water, then gently squeeze out the excess moisture and reshape the bristles before storing.
- Oil-Based Paint: Pour a small amount of mineral spirits or paint thinner into a container, then swirl the brush or roller in the solution until the paint is dissolved. Use a brush comb or your fingers to remove any remaining paint, then rinse the brush or roller with warm, soapy water and let it air dry before storing.

8. How long does interior paint typically last?

The lifespan of interior paint depends on several factors, including the quality of the paint, the surface it's applied to, and the amount of wear and tear it receives. On average, interior paint can last anywhere from 5-10 years before it starts to show signs of fading, chipping, or peeling. However, high-traffic areas like kitchens and bathrooms may need to be repainted more frequently, while low-traffic areas like bedrooms and living rooms may last longer. To extend the life of your interior paint, be sure to:

- Choose a high-quality, durable paint that is suitable for the room's function and level of use.
- Prepare the surface properly before painting, including cleaning, repairing, and priming as needed.
- Apply the paint in thin, even coats, allowing each coat to dry completely before applying the next.
- Maintain the painted surface by cleaning it regularly and touching up any chips, cracks, or other damage as soon as possible.

By keeping these frequently asked questions and answers in mind, you'll be well-prepared to tackle your interior painting project with confidence and skill. Remember, the key to a successful paint job is patience, preparation, and attention to detail. Take your time, do your research, and don't be afraid to ask for help or guidance when needed. With a little knowledge and a lot of determination, you can transform any room in your home into a beautiful, personalized space that you'll love for years to come. Happy painting!

Conclusion

Congratulations! You've made it through the ultimate DIY guide to transforming your living space with expert interior painting techniques, color schemes, and essential tools. By now, you should have a solid understanding of the entire painting process, from selecting the perfect color palette to applying the final finishing touches.

Throughout this book, we've covered everything you need to know to achieve professional-quality results, including:

1. Preparing your space by clearing the room, protecting surfaces, and repairing imperfections.
2. Choosing the right tools and supplies, such as brushes, rollers, and paint types.
3. Mastering essential painting techniques, like cutting in, rolling, and creating special effects.
4. Selecting colors that reflect your personal style and create the desired mood in each room.
5. Troubleshooting common painting challenges and avoiding mistakes.

Armed with this knowledge and your newfound skills, you're ready to take on any interior painting project with confidence and ease. Whether you're looking to refresh a single room or tackle a whole-house makeover, you have the power to create a space that truly reflects your unique personality and style.

But the benefits of painting your home interior go beyond just aesthetics. A fresh coat of paint can also:

1. Increase the value of your home by making it more attractive to potential buyers.

2. Protect your walls from everyday wear and tear, extending their lifespan and saving you money on repairs.

3. Improve your mood and well-being by creating a more inviting, relaxing atmosphere.

4. Express your creativity and personal taste, making your house feel more like a true home.

So don't be afraid to experiment, take risks, and think outside the box when it comes to your interior painting projects. With a little imagination and a lot of heart, you can transform even the most mundane spaces into something truly extraordinary.

As you step back and admire your newly painted rooms, take a moment to reflect on all the hard work, dedication, and care that went into each brushstroke. Feel proud of what you've accomplished, and enjoy the sense of satisfaction that comes with creating something beautiful with your own two hands.

And remember, painting is not just a one-time project, but a lifelong journey of self-expression and home improvement. As your tastes and needs change over time, you can always revisit this guide and use your skills to update and refresh your space, keeping it feeling fresh, modern, and uniquely you.

So go ahead, grab your brushes, and start making your mark on the world, one wall at a time. The only limit is your imagination, and with this ultimate DIY guide by your side, the possibilities are truly endless. Happy painting!

www.ingramcontent.com/pod-product-compliance
Lightning Source LLC
Chambersburg PA
CBHW050821250726
48653CB00006B/2360